MW00414535

Benedictions

Christmas 2017

For Josette,

A wonderfully written, inspirational book by my own dear sister!

Enjoy!

Laurie and Peter

Benedictions

26 Reflections

Julie K. Aageson

WIPF & STOCK · Eugene, Oregon

Wipf & Stock
An Imprint of Wipf and Stock Publishers
199 W. 8th Ave., Suite 3
Eugene, OR 97401

www.wipfandstock.com

PAPERBACK ISBN 13: 978-1-4982-7959-8
HARDCOVER ISBN 13: 978-1-4982-7961-1

Manufactured in the U.S.A.   02/22/2016

With much love and gratitude for Jim
whose steady presence and patient partnership
continue to be lifelong benedictions.

Contents

Permissions

1 Holy Ground, p. 4. Poem *Holy Ground* by Veronica Koperski. Used with permission of the author and of The Liturgical Conference. First published in *Liturgy* 9.3 (1991) 63.

9 Liturgy, p. 29. Use of the line from "Now the feast and celebration, all of creation sings for joy." Haugen, "Now the Feast," 1990, GIA. All rights reserved. Used with permission.

12 Real Life, p. 38. Quote by Deborah K. Cronin in *Holy Ground: Celtic Christian Spirituality*. Used with permission.

17 Music, p. 53. "For the Beauty of the Earth." Text by Folliott S. Pierpoint. This is in the public domain.

17 Music, p. 54. "Go, My Children, with My Blessing." Text by Jaroslav Vajda. St. Louis, CPH, 1983. Used with permission.

17 Music, p. 54. "Shepherd Me, O God." Text by Marty Haugen. Based on Psalm 23. Used with permission. All rights reserved.

20 Learning to be *We*, p. 62. "As the Grains of Wheat." Text from Didache, 2nd century; Marty Haugen. GIA, 1990. Used with permission. All rights reserved.

20 Learning to be *We*, p. 64. "One Bread, One Body." Text by John
B. Foley. OCP, 1978. All rights reserved. Used with permission.

22 Singers of Life, p. 68. Loren Eiseley, *The Immense Journey*.
Random House, 1956. I found it in *Creative Brooding* by Robert
Raines. New York: Macmillan, 1967. Used with permission. 1946.

23 Hunger and Thirst, p. 72. John Shea, *Stories of Faith*. Quote used
with permission of the author and of Father Gregory Pierce, editor,
president, and publisher of ACTA.

Overview

Benedictions is a collection of reflections about the presence of the sacred in ordinary things. In the everyday experiences described here, God's presence is palpable, tangible, real. "Cleave the wood and I am there," says Isaiah in the apocryphal *Gospel of Thomas*. "Lift up the stone, and you will find me there." These benedictions—literally good words, blessings, tastes of God—remind readers to live life with feeling and passion and art, paying attention to the holiness of the commonplace: the ground beneath our feet, the ways we bless each other, loss and grief and the making of our homes, or in the words of Gertrud Mueller Nelson, the paper scraps, sticks and rags and soups, sunrises and compost piles, the stuff of which we spin an atmosphere for family, neighbors, and friends, without which there is no taste of God.

Many of us spend a lifetime looking for God's face. The introduction to *Benedictions* sets the stage for my own search by describing the place of my childhood and how it shaped my first experiences of God's presence. In the reflections that follow, I write about places and people, seasons of life and seasons of experience that show readers God's face in the journey that is life. There is a vastness, a spaciousness about the meanings of God that I sensed even as a young child experiencing the daily ebbing and flooding of the tides and the nightly wonders of the universe. My hope is that readers will discover their own benedictions here in the wonder and mystery of God's holy presence.

Introduction

The object of life is to live it with feeling and passion and art—minutely—because without the paper scraps, the sticks and rags and soups, without sunrises or compost piles, without babies and loves, without spinning an atmosphere for family, neighbors, and friends, there is no taste of God.[1]

At the topmost corner of the western United States, a beautifully unspoiled chain of islands lie jewel-like between the southern tip of Canada's Vancouver Island and the ragged coastline of the US mainland. More than two hundred of these islands form a long archipelago leading from the northern end of Puget Sound out into the straits of Rosario, Haro, and Georgia. Through the sometimes narrow and circuitous channels, waterways and straits that separate the mostly high-cliffed, tree-covered islands, saltwater tides ebb and flood. In their wake, shell-strewn beaches lie crisscrossed with endless varieties of saltwater creatures and odd assortments of driftwood and logs washed clean several times each day by the clockwork regularity of tides.

I spent my childhood on one of these small islands, tucked between the majestic peaks of the Cascade Mountains on the mainland and the ragtag assortment of adjacent islands scattered across the sound. Our world was framed by the geography that defines this extraordinarily beautiful area of the Pacific Northwest.

1. Mueller Nelson, *Here All Dwell Free*, 91.

1

The names of the islands closest to us—Orcas, Cypress, Sinclair, Eliza, Vendovi, Samish, Jack—roll off my tongue like old familiar friends. Great ships and barges, tankers and ferries plied the waterways and channels between the islands, bringing oil to inland refineries and—from the vantage of childhood anyway—mysterious and exotic goods from foreign ports. In the fog-shrouded channels, the deep resonance of ship horns and sharp whistles and buoy bells clanging in the mist signaled faraway places and the lure of a bigger world beyond.

In that pristine and unspoiled place where old-growth fir and cedar tower high above the beaches and sometimes fall like matchsticks in high winds, I spent summer days exploring the shoreline searching for the agates we saved like nuggets of gold, waiting for low tide to uncover masses of small, scurrying rock crabs beneath shiny wet beach gravel, and making imaginary houses up among the driftwood where the green, tender moss covering the backsides of the damp logs made soft carpets.

Daily forays on the water took place in an old dilapidated skiff which floated away regularly with the tide, oars askew, later to be found down the beach bobbing against the shore. Much later, my grandfather built a new wooden boat weighing what felt like a ton in hopes, I suspect, that a heavier skiff would better withstand the forgetfulness of children. In those boats and numerous others built by my father, we dallied out among the kelp beds and along the bay probing the mysteries beneath us in the shallow places where schools of herring and candlefish play. When we ventured out in the deep water, crossing choppy channels to explore other islands, I tried to visualize the unknown depths. On stormy days with the tide ripping and swirling around us, I was both curious about the riddles and fearful of the dark fathoms beneath me.

With the coming of night and the vast canopy of the heavens all around, curiosity and awe over the size of the universe and the wonder of creation were my constant companions. In the silence of the night—deep quiet broken only by bird sounds and the steady lapping of the waves against the shore, the grand expanses of stars and planets strewn across the night sky stirred a compelling sense of the mystery of God. On that beach among the sounds and smells and sights, in the rhythms of the tides and the cycles of the days and seasons, I began to learn about living life with feeling and passion and art. And though the ensuing years have taken me far from my childhood island world, the beauty and wonder of that place remain deep in my being, still shaping today the way in which I look at the world—a benediction for living life mindfully.

Many of us spend a lifetime looking for God's face. And if we are honest, we don't begin to understand the ins and outs of who God is and how God works. I do know that this place of my childhood shaped my first experiences of God's presence. Every year and at an ever faster pace, my sense of the wonder and mystery of God seems to grow exponentially. There is a vastness, a spaciousness about the meanings of God that I sensed even as a young child experiencing the daily ebbing and flooding of the tides and the nightly wonders of the universe.

Benedictions is a collection of reflections about the holiness of ordinary things. In these everyday experiences, God is present, tangible, real. "Cleave the wood and I am there," says Isaiah in the apocryphal *Gospel of Thomas*. "Lift up the stone, and you will find me there." *Benedictions* is about living with feeling and passion and art, paying attention to the holiness of the ordinary—paper scraps, sticks and rags and soups, sunrises and compost piles, the stuff of which we spin an atmosphere for family, neighbors, and friends, without which there is no taste of God.[2] These benedictions—literally good words, blessings, tastes of God—remind us that "sun and stars and souls do not ramble in a vacuum"[3] and that God and God's spirit continue to accompany all of us in the journey that is life. May these words be life-giving and grace-filled benedictions for you.

2. Ibid.
3. Heschel, *Man Is Not Alone*, 76.

1

Holy Ground

I shall seek no longer for the burning bush;
All bushes are ablaze.
And I will not hasten to depart
From daily grief and gladness
To climb a holy mountain;
Every mountain now is sacred,
Each marketplace and every home,
All, all are blessed
Since God has pitched a tent among us.

Now on our earth are to be found
The footprints of the Word made flesh
Who walked with us in wind and rain
And under sun and stars,
In joy and sorrow,
Born of Mary, watched over by Joseph,
Eating and drinking, living and loving.

Dying yet living, the Word made flesh
All, all the earth
And each of us
Is holy ground
Where we must slip our sandals off
and walk softly, filled with wonder.[1]

1. Koperski, "Holy Ground," 63.

4

There are a thousand ways to kneel and kiss the earth. Believing that we walk on holy ground and that we ourselves are holy ground magnifies the reverence and awe Sufi poet Rumi expresses for our fragile planet, our fragile lives. "Kiss the ground for me," I say longingly to a friend on her way home to the Pacific Northwest where I grew up. It's the deep of winter where I live and the cold and snow have taken their toll. To cope, I'm remembering the smell of damp earth and the feel of soft winter rain, misty fog, and the rhythm of saltwater tides washing in and out over the course of every day. Asking a friend to pay homage to my childhood home is a way of acknowledging a place and a time that nurtures and enriches my life. It's the holy ground that gave me birth and set me on my way. It's the place where I was introduced to a loving and generous God.

A young pastor speaks of holy ground when she steps into the pulpit. She knows that the words she proclaims and the presence of God's spirit come together there to bear life and healing to hearers who are hungry, thirsty, broken. So keenly does she feel this that she always removes her shoes before standing in that sacred place, on that holy ground.

Tomorrow my spouse and I will help serve the evening meal at a nearby homeless shelter. In this place of broken lives and spirits, I come away knowing that Christ is present—in the eyes of those who receive and in the eyes of those who serve, eyes which are not distinguishable one from the other. We all come hungry, broken. Sacred space, holy ground.

In her book *An Altar in the World*, Barbara Brown Taylor ponders God's presence in the world, even wondering where we get the impression that God is primarily interested in religion. Or that God's home is the church? Or that the world is a barren place to be rejected in exchange for heaven? Again and again, Taylor speaks of the whole world as the house of God. She reminds us that God is present here, now; that holy ground is to be found in the ordinary stuff of life; and that when we pay attention, we notice God in one another and in all of creation.

Where we are is where God is. God graces us by hallowing the ordinary places where we live and work and share daily life. Our relationships, our life in community, the natural world around us—all are holy ground!

Notice the holy ground where you live. Recognize wellsprings of grace in the everyday, commonplace rituals of life. Pay attention to God's spirit in the people you meet. Celebrate the ordinary rhythms of your life. Think of ways you might kneel and kiss the earth.

REFLECTION

The whole world is the house of God and all, all are blessed since God has pitched a tent among us.

* Where are the places you call holy?

* Where do you kneel to express gratitude or to kiss the earth?

* Like Moses, do you need to be reminded that beside the burning bush, right where *you* are, the place where *you* stand, is holy?

* What does it mean that where you are is where God is?

2

Home

In the summer when we were children, we often slept outside in a roomy white canvas tent we'd converted into a bedroom. A tattered old Oriental carpet defined the space beneath two quilt-covered double beds and two single beds lined up against the four canvas walls. My sisters and I made the tent our very own summer home and on warm island afternoons, lounging lazily on the sagging beds, we read endless stacks of books sometimes falling asleep in the comforting warmth of the tent to dream about the intrigues of the stories that so captured our imaginations.

An adjacent log cabin was another home. Some of my most vivid memories from childhood are framed by that sturdy one-room cabin built by my father and grandfather and perched above the beach where the coming and going of daily tides shaped our playground. No matter where I am, I can conjure up the smell and the feel of that log cabin so redolent with scents of cedar and fir.

My dreams of this island home are often oddly disjointed—familiar people juxtaposed with strange arrangements of the beach, the cabins, and passing boats and ships. Once I dreamed that an airliner swooped out of the sky careening into the trees and the hillside above the cabin, an omen perhaps of family brokenness we could not see then. In dreams and in real life, always there are tug boats and row boats and ferries coming and going in rhythms like the tides they try to catch. Sometimes they are anchored out among the islands and in my dreams they take on mythic size and meaning. The island is among the first of my homes, treasured now as a memory.

Another of these is the "house at 2012," a big, rambling arts and crafts–style home where my grandparents lived. How many times I have dreamed of this house—of my grandmother's garden, of the back stairs cloaked always in that childhood remembrance of fear of the dark, of the spigot on the very long bathtub in the tiled "big bathroom" at the back of the house, of the attic where we spent hours exploring among the rafters in old trunks and boxes. My great-grandmother lived for most of my childhood in an apartment at the back of that long, sprawling house and I can still hear the creaking sound of the angled door as it opened into her living room where an old pump organ held forth. The whole house seemed filled with stories of the past—oddly interesting furniture and secret spaces inherited from former owners whose ginseng business evoked exotic images of China and what we then called the Orient.

The house at 2012 became home—the gathering place—for extended family. On Sunday afternoons around tables laden with garlic-studded roast beef, mashed potatoes with rich brown gravy, garden vegetables and homemade pickles, relatives came from near and far to feast and share stories. As the afternoon progressed and before people began to think about leaving, my grandfather would line everyone up between the two apple trees in the front yard: the smallest children sitting on the ground, gawky, awkward adolescents behind them, and adults both tall and short filling in all the gaps, at least three deep, sometimes thirty or forty of us posing *just one more time.*

These places where I first learned the meaning of home continue to shape my life. They are benedictions—holy ground—and the places where I learned who I was and who God is. They became a set of interconnected experiences where I felt the love of parents and siblings and extended family. They introduced me to "my people" and to our unique history. And they provided a foundation for future homes, a cradle that would both anchor life and allow it to move forward into the future.

Home—and the benediction of home, and all its meanings—always is characterized by joy and sorrow, grief and gladness, complex combinations of the realities of complicated lives. It's where we come from and it shapes where we are going. Home is sacred and from its walls we can all go forth, no longer seeking the burning bush or the holy mountain but knowing that we are blessed *here*, that God is present *here*, that we are home because God, our true home, has indeed pitched a tent among us. We are God's dwelling place. We are God's home.

REFLECTION

We are God's dwelling place. We are God's home.

* Where are the places you call home?
* What are some of the ways these places nurture you?
* What does it mean to you that we are God's dwelling place?
* How might home be a description for God?

3

Saint Andrew's Church

Anne Lamott is one of my favorite writers. She's a truth-teller—brutally honest, irreverent, funny, someone who knows that life can be filled with torturous challenges, a woman both vulnerable and steely strong. I will never forget the images in her book *Traveling Mercies: Some Thoughts on Faith*, describing her experience of becoming a Christian.

I use these words—"becoming a Christian"—cautiously. Sometimes there is an off-putting piety about them that feels self-righteous or at worst, self-serving. But Lamott is anything but pious. And despite earlier encounters with Christians and Christianity that have left a bad taste, she writes eloquently about being pursued by God and embraced by Christianity.

Her bohemian life of broken relationships, addictions, and an empty search for meaning careen out of control until one day, everything comes unraveled. In the tormented darkness of physical and mental anguish and drug and alcohol dependency, Lamott imagines the presence of a little cat. She knows this presence to be Jesus, waiting without intruding to offer comfort, healing, acceptance, and unconditional love—the shelter of God's wings, benediction.

What should *not* be amazing is that Lamott finds a small church in Marin City, California, where all twenty-three members embrace and welcome her. Embodying the love of Christ and seeing in her their own brokenness and frailty, they welcome her "home" and provide a shelter for her, a respite from the chaos of her life. They welcome her to a community, to a place where all are welcome, a place devoted to caring for others.

Now many years later, Lamott still writes regularly about Saint Andrew's Church. When I hear occasional stories of churches worshiping thousands of people every Sunday or baptizing 539 new members at Eastertime, when I drive by the Canvas Church and the Skull Church and the Church for Cowboys on my way to the smaller place where I worship, I think of Saint Andrew's. It's hardly successful if one counts numbers or baptisms or weekly programs. But it is a place of shelter for all twenty-three people who worship there because they welcome one another in mercy and love. They struggle financially, they never know if they will be able to pay their pastor or priest, they don't seem to attract crowds. Anne Lamott teaches the children at Saint Andrew's in a one-room Sunday school.

Lamott goes to Saint Andrew's because she finds nourishment there. She has found in its people a God of mercy and love, a God who saves us from ourselves and calls each of us to make a difference in the world. She goes to Saint Andrew's because she encounters a living God in that place, a God who helps make sense of a sometimes senseless world. She describes Saint Andrew's as a kind of safe house, an anchor in the storm, a refuge. It serves as a compass and a lens for wending her way through life.

On occasional Sunday mornings when I am tempted to worship at altars of my own, I think about our common need for community and the shared graces of word, water, wine and bread. I am reminded of the body of Christ that is about the *we and the us* rather than the *I and the me*. I remember how clearly we all need places of mercy, reminders of forgiveness and healing, grace.

Anne Lamott went to church twice last Sunday. She doesn't share this to sound churchy or pious. She tells us because church

is where she finds real food, living water, hope, and shelter from
the storms that plague us all. She celebrates having been at church
because she meets Christ there. In the company of the body of
Christ, she finds ways of seeing Christ in herself and others and
of being Christ to the chaotic world all around us. Saint Andrew's
and its people live in the shelter of each other which is to say they
understand what it means to be the body of Christ. May such a
benediction be true for us as well.

REFLECTION

Saint Andrew's is a kind of safe house, an anchor in the storm, a
refuge.

*   Where do you find real food, living water, hope, and shelter
    from the storms of life?

*   What seem to be some marks of successful churches in our
    culture?

*   How might our churches become safe houses, anchors,
    shelters?

*   What does "being church" mean to you?

*   Why does it seem to be so difficult?

4

Bread of Life

Plastic bags filled with rounds of leftover pita bread can be seen in the oddest places: stuck between cracks in the walls of Jerusalem's Old City, hanging from a door leading through a winding back alley in the West Bank, strewn atop a rock wall on the Mount of Olives where nothing will disturb the holy bread except hunger. In some places in the Middle East, bread is so revered—so symbolic—that what is left over is never thrown away, never discarded to become garbage underfoot. The extra loaves and rounds are placed in public spaces where someone hungry might find nourishment, the bread of life. Bread is holy.

Bread is a staple of life. Among my earliest memories of home is the unforgettable smell of freshly baked bread. I loved its distinctive taste and simple beauty, the variety of shapes and sizes, the designs cut into the tops of each loaf, the way it signified something more than nourishment. When I learned to make bread myself, I liked experimenting with my mother's best recipes: jule kaga, Swedish rye, orange rolls, and more. Most of all, it was deeply gratifying to offer bread to others, to share the bounty, to break bread together.

Bethlehem, the city of Christ's birth, is a Hebrew word meaning "house of bread." The Christ-child's birthplace is a manger, the French verb for "to eat." What kind of benediction is this? Is Jesus truly the bread of life? What does it mean that Jesus comes to us in a manger used as a feedbox or that we place his birth in a small town named house of bread? What does it mean that we receive Christ's body in the form of bread and wine or that we are called to be the body of Christ, bread for the world? Is Christianity, Christian life, about food and drink? What does Jesus have to do with hunger? Can hunger be both physical and spiritual?

There is something primal and basic about bread. Whether tortillas warm from a hot griddle, lefse rolled paper thin and spread with butter, sugar and cinnamon, manna in the wilderness or simply food for our own tables, bread is connected to the longing we all have to eat and be satisfied. Bread is holy.

In the same way, Jesus—and all we believe Jesus to be—is bread for our lives. His life and his death are about feeding one another, caring for one another, inviting one another to feast on the bread of life.

In the parables he taught and in the life he lived, we see this Jesus to be bread for the world incarnate in each of us. He comes to us and through us, a benediction nourishing our bodies as well as our souls, asking us to be bread for the world. May the Bread of Life find a place at our tables, in our mangers, on our doorposts, in our homes. And may we who have bread in abundance—enough to feed the world—share this bread of life beyond our own tables, our own communities, and our own "kind."

Holy God, you are the bread of life, our table and our food, a holy benediction.

REFLECTION

May the Bread of Life find a place at our tables, in our mangers, on our doorposts, in our homes.

* What are your earliest memories of bread?

* What are some ways we might connect ordinary bread to the bread of the Eucharist?

* Bread, a holy benediction—another name for God? How?

* Read the bread texts in the Gospel of John.

5

Seeing through a Mirror Dimly

Where even to begin? How to confess all the ways one wrestles with the feeble constructs we assemble to help us understand who God is, what God means? How to express faith without drawing from old containers filled with words and phrases and doctrines no longer helpful? How to live with so many questions, less certitude, so much ambiguity? Seeing through a mirror dimly? Oh yes.

I well remember the late-night discussions in my university dorm room about original sin, "the fall," salvation, heaven and hell, atonement, justification . . . we had so many answers. Perhaps some of these theological windows were helpful if only for their ability to stimulate conversation and provoke thoughtful grappling.

German theologian Paul Tillich liked to speak of faith as a window, a lens for looking at the world. He challenged students to consider the Bible, prayer, even Jesus as windows. He warned against making the window, the glass—whether Scripture, prayer, or our own traditions—the objects of our devotion. Tillich was adamant about all these things pointing to God and a way of looking at the world.

Especially in matters of faith, I often see through a mirror dimly. The containers of Christian certainties, once so well defined and articulated with such confidence, are inadequate and have lost their power to persuade. I am grateful for a tradition that avoids biblical literalism and fundamentalism to make room for questions, mystery, even uncertainty. I appreciate compelling, dynamic faith and at the same time find authenticity and truthfulness in partial pictures, inadequate definitions, ongoing wrestling.

This willingness to live with mystery makes me wary of nicely turned descriptions about who Jesus was, who God is, or what it means to be Christian. I am certain that none of the great religions of the world has a corner on truth and I am equally certain that God is bigger than our creeds and confessions and nailed-down attempts at definitive answers.

Another Paul, the apostle, wrote comforting words in 1 Corinthians: "For now we see in a mirror dimly . . . now I know only in part." This Paul is also a window, another lens for helping us live with mystery, without easy answers and pious phrases and neat definitions. He too wrestles with questions and uncertainties and invites us to see the world through the eyes of Christ.

Always the skeptic, I don't mind living with questions of faith. I don't find many crystal clear windows and I don't mind smudges. There is freedom in admitting our inadequate attempts to define God, perhaps even some relief over knowing that we do not know. This is part of the dynamism and mystery of faith.

Even so, the smudged windows and dimly lit mirrors provide a view of the world that makes sense to me. Through this changing panoply of lenses, as convoluted or limiting as they may be, I see a life-giving, generous God who continues creating and birthing and surprising us with one another and with a universe we don't begin to comprehend.

Through these dim mirrors, the ordinary things of life—daily routine, family relationships, unexpected illness and loss, the steady beat of world events, the cycles of nature, our own self-absorption—are transformed into something more than ordinary. Seen through the smudged windows and mirrors, each of these commonplace things becomes a vessel for showing us God's over-whelming love and grace, helping us bear everyday witness to the workings of God. A benediction indeed!

REFLECTION

Especially in matters of faith, I often see through a mirror dimly. The containers of Christian certainties, once so well defined and articulated with such confidence, are inadequate.

* Why (or why not) does it seem difficult for us to express doubt about belief or about matters of faith?

* Do you recall particular words or doctrines that for you were once meaningful but no longer seem helpful?

* Can Christians wrestle with meaning and belief to see it as life giving?

* How do our feeble attempts to define God show a willingness to live with mystery?

6

Discussion

A flamboyantly colorful African painting by Ugandan artist Paul Nzalamba hangs on the wall in my study. Three African women are shown deep in conversation, wholly absorbed with each other's presence. Wearing vibrantly patterned dresses with matching head wraps each of a different design, they seem to sway in an aura of energy as arms wave and heads nod. The intensity of the painting and the power of the images shout of collaboration, shared passion, sisterhood. Whatever they are discussing has them spellbound, sitting on the very edges of their seats, totally engrossed in the topic of the moment. Nzalamba has named the painting *Discussion*.

This painting hangs opposite another striking image and description of a young girl with dark purple hair panhandling outside a Holiday Inn. It's a cold winter morning and she's holding a baby. When a hotel employee steps outside to ask her to leave, the artist asks the question, "I wonder if anyone would recognize the Christ-child if they happened to meet?"

The placement of these two provocative images is not accidental. Neither are the themes they each represent. Shortly after I moved into my new study, a sister-in-law came to visit. As we sat together beneath these two pictures, Carrie described to me a woman who appeared at her church one evening during a catechism class. The woman was asking for help, for money and a place to stay while making her way to a city where promising jobs might make her life more tolerable. Carrie and I spent the next hour or two discussing the impact of this woman on the confirmation students and on a sister-in-law hungry herself for living more deeply, for learning to embrace strangers and welcome outsiders.

Back to my study. On the bookshelves below the three African women in *Discussion* sits a little Peruvian sculpture of another woman surrounded by children. They cling to her shoulders and arms, spilling over into her lap and onto her feet. She is reading to them as they try desperately to get close to her and to the story she shares. When the story ends, I imagine questions and conversation, a discussion that has been repeated since time began.

On the window shelves above my desk is a stunning piece of blown glass, a small vase with red and brown rivulets of color streaming through it. It too is a gift from a friend with whom I have shared conversation and discussion for years. Our visits began during a difficult pregnancy. We read together then, sharing readings from a collection of spiritual classics. It was a way of getting to know one another and a way for my friend to endure a long pregnancy. Later, when her son was diagnosed with autism, there were many more discussions. A proud mother learned to share her son's gift of creativity. The son became a friend—"Hello, Jim. Hello, Julie"—always said in the same mechanical tone of predictability and good manners and always received with gratitude.

The lovely blown glass vase in my windowsill embodies the fragility of life and the care of a friend who when I moved far away, threw a farewell party inviting neighbors for rich conversation and chocolate raspberry torte fit for a gourmet magazine—benedictions all.

Carved wooden tulips and silk yellow and blue pansies also sit above my desk in a crooked piece of pottery. They aren't remarkable in any way but they come from one of many trips taken with my sisters. I keep them because they remind me of my family and our lifelong discussions, our memories, the joys and sorrows we share. The crooked pottery is from another friend, a colleague who has come to stay with us many times, always bringing a thoughtful gift. How many, many discussions we've had with Jim—afternoon conversations with tea one winter in Crete, watching movies together in the pine-paneled room in his home in Minnesota, Easter dinner in the same lovely Tudor house where his collection of Ukrainian Easter eggs formed the centerpiece of a table laden with Greek food and an atmosphere marked by discussion and good conversation.

Conversation and discussion are benedictions drawing us closer to one another and allowing us to see beneath the surface of things. They remind us to live life with feeling and passion and art, paying attention to the holiness of common things—the ground beneath our feet, the ways we bless each other, loss and grief and the making of our homes, the ordinary things of life turned into benedictions of blessing.

REFLECTION

Conversation and discussion are benedictions drawing us closer to one another and allowing us to see beneath the surface of things.

* Where are the places for conversation that most satisfy you?

* What makes a discussion worthwhile or life-giving?

* What does it mean to you to live life with feeling and passion and art, paying attention to the holiness of common things?

7

Beauty as Benediction

It isn't accidental that this collection of reflections begins with a description of my childhood home, a place of astonishing natural beauty. It was there that the beginnings of a sense of the sacred were stirred for me by daily interaction with the natural world. Now many decades later, I've made homes in places with their own distinctive geography, nearly always finding beauty very different from my childhood home—wide-open prairie spaces, the rolling hills and lakes of the Midwest, urban cities and the lush green countryside of England.

I don't begin to understand the puzzle of God or how God works. The sacred presence is an unending mystery but today as I walk along a rushing river twisting its way through canyons and around bends defined by the spectacular Rocky Mountains still wearing white crowns of snow in the middle of summer, I sense the vastness of God and the spaciousness of God's meanings.

A year ago this summer, my spouse and I hiked into the back country of Glacier National Park to do some exploring with a seasoned old park ranger. This soft-spoken, lean and lanky naturalist wasn't particularly polished or articulate. But when he began to describe the flora and the fauna and the geography of this place, he became a poet, a musician, an artist. He was offering us a blessing, a glimpse of the creation that still captivates him even at the end of a long career and endless days walking steep and circuitous mountain trails.

As we hiked the face of the Going-to-the-Sun Road and then on up into a basin at the very top of the Garden Wall, the ranger pointed out every delicate wild flower, million-year-old striations in the rock formations, large and small birds, clambering mountain goats on a hillside in the distance, elegant bighorn sheep, gnarled trees, a grizzly grazing in a meadow far below where only yards away, a couple of deer played together. It was a breathtaking feast of beauty.

That evening around the fire in the stone shelter at Granite Park, our ranger described a night of terror many years ago when, largely due to inattention to wildlife management, two people were killed by bears. He told the story because he had been there to witness the tragedy. He also told the story as a teacher, one who reveres God's creation, one who sees the connectedness and beauty of life and our responsibility to it. He told the story to help us better see and understand and respect the natural world and he told the story so no one would forget the suffering of that day fifty years ago.

Each of us experiences beauty in thousands of different ways. I think of the powerful beauty of a single voice singing from the depths of the collapsing earth as a Haitian earthquake buried him beneath the rubble. It was a moment of overwhelming sorrow and loss. But it was also a moment of affirmation that nothing, not floods or famine or earthquakes or broken relationships—nothing—can separate us from the love of God. Beauty in the midst of unspeakable horror, a benediction, God in the midst of death and life.

Not long ago, a friend shared with me a photo of an early morning sunrise. The picture was titled *Begin with Yes*, reminding me of a reflection by twentieth-century psychiatrist Viktor Frankl. Frankl described being at work in a trench, the ravages of war dark and broken all around him. As he struggled to find the reason

for such suffering and hopelessness, he sensed his spirit pierc-
ing through the gloom with a resounding *yes* in the face of what
seemed to be a meaningless world. At the same time, a light came
on in a distant farmhouse on the gray horizon affirming Frankl's
yes, affirming God's *yes*.

A benediction is God's *yes*. God is present everywhere we
look: in the world of nature filled with beauty and terror, in the
rubble of natural disasters, in the darkness of despair. God's *yes* is
beauty itself.

REFLECTION

He was offering us a blessing, a glimpse of the creation that still
captivated him even at the end of a long career and endless days
walking mountain trails.

* What might it mean that a benediction is God's *yes?*

* What are some ways the beauty of the natural world speaks
  to you?

* Have you or someone you know experienced tragedy or loss
  that in some ways becomes a moment of affirmation?

* How do you imagine the mystery of God's presence? Is it
  spacious?

8

Quotidian Mercies

The object of life is to live it with feeling and passion and art—minutely—because without the paper scraps, the sticks and rags and soups, without sunrises or compost piles, without babies and loves, without spinning an atmosphere for family, neighbors, and friends, there is no taste of God.[1]

I sat with the moon this morning. Cup of tea in hand and the house still for a moment, I watched its slow waning in the early morning light feeling a sense of camaraderie and appreciation for the steady presence of this subtle and radiant orb, so much a part of the landscape as to make us take it for granted. But this morning I was not taking it for granted.

In the stillness and peace of early morning, the contentment I felt was about ordinary things. Peaches we'd picked and frozen in lovely, golden chunks for winter breakfasts, a reminder of mid-summer sunshine and orchards hanging heavy with the fragrant smell of ripened fruit. Coffee stains on an already dirty carpet reminding me of daughters and their little ones home for vacation and unconcerned about trivialities like spilled coffee. Green grass

---

1. Mueller Nelson, *Here All Dwell Free*, 91.

in need of mowing and towering mountains and a home that holds us in its warm embrace.

The moon and I began to fade as children paddled down the stairs, eyes still heavy from sleep, hungry and looking for breakfast. Upstairs a baby cried and outside and at a distance, I could hear the shuttering vibrations of a morning train rumbling through our small village on its journey east. The moon now low on the western horizon slowly dwindled from view still holding me in its thrall, my tea cup needing a refill and the nonstop activity of another day pulling me away from reverie into reality.

My pantry is stocked, my freezer is full. There are no enemy troops at the gates of our comfortable lives and the moon is my steady companion. But even the moon wanes away and out of sight for three days each month, and the inky darkness of a moonless night reminds me of the darkness of the world. This same iridescent moon that sits with me on a quiet morning waned earlier today over a mother nursing a newly born child as she huddled with sixty or seventy other refugees in a leaking rubber raft, all of them fleeing from the ravages of war-torn Syria. It shines down to illuminate the rubble of a white-walled Palestinian city where yesterday two young boys were shot and killed as they walked to school. It hovers above a neighborhood in Charleston, South Carolina, where families will grieve the rest of their lives for loved ones gunned down while sitting together in a church.

The quotidian mercies I find so comforting—daily life with family, the rhythms of the seasons, the patterns of the church year, cooking and cleaning and creating a home, safety—easily become expected routines of entitlement. I like to describe them as tastes of God, holy expressions of God's presence in everyday life. The riches of the goodness of God taken, if not for granted, as signs of God's love and mercy.

But in the darkness of the three days, on moonless nights, seeing the face of God is not so easy. Walking this morning with my spouse, leaves crunching under our feet in the crisp air of fall, I also walk with a long, meandering line of immigrants hoping to escape the terror of drug lords. Watching another mind-numbing (and oddly captivating) television program about which house to love or which house to sell or how to renovate already livable space, I remember Gaza where after another full-scale attack on its already disintegrating existence, no homes have been rebuilt and quotidian mercies are few and far between.

Awaken us, O God, to your face in the daily ordinariness of life. Keep us from self-satisfied basking in feel-good Christianity. Save us from self-absorption, too much contentment, and the presumptuous lie of entitlement. Help us see you in the darkness when there is no moon. Show us how to roll away stones that imprison and stones that kill. Teach us to sit with the moon and help us engage with darkness. Show us your face, holy God, in the everyday, the commonplace, the benediction of your presence.

REFLECTION

The quotidian mercies I find so comforting—daily life with family, the rhythms of the seasons, the patterns of the church year, cooking and cleaning and creating a home, safety—easily become expected routines of entitlement.

* Finding balance between gratitude for everyday life and engagement with the darkness of the world is a lifelong challenge. How does this happen?

* How do we avoid the traps of our self-satisfied culture?

* When did you last sit with the moon?

9

Liturgy

On the Saturday night before Easter—Holy Saturday in the Christian tradition—we gather outside the entrance to our church to light a fire against the chill of the evening and the coming of night. Lent is over, the three-day Triduum has begun, and we've come to reenact the mysteries of life and death and resurrection. Lighting the tall, beautifully marked ivory paschal candle from a fire pit and holding the heavy beeswax candle high, a cantor's resonant voice solemnly proclaims, "The light of Christ," and a parade of worshipers, winter-weary and longing for Easter, call back, "Thanks be to God," as they slowly process into the dark cavern of the sanctuary. Again, the rich voice of the cantor calls out more loudly now, "The light of Christ," and again the ragtag group responds, "Thanks be to God." The flickering light of the paschal candle casts shadows and then more and more candles are lit as the stories of God's saving acts are told in song and text and prayer. Slowly, the deep darkness of the womb-like sanctuary begins to dissipate.

In that candle-lit cavern of a church, we listen and watch as the saving stories of God's overwhelming love for humankind are told and illustrated. We hear the drama of creation, the sorry saga of the flood and Noah's obedience, of the Valley of Bones where Ezekiel describes so vividly the dry bones coming together, bone upon bone, taking on flesh, breathing in the breath of God, coming to life. They are our stories, our drama, our journeys. In this night of nights, we experience the saga of God's covenant with God's people. It's the necessary backdrop for helping us know and experience resurrection and Easter.

I have been shaped by the liturgy. From early memories of worship in my tradition, it was the preacher and the sermon that counted most and merited rigorous critique and rating. The liturgy belonged to all of us. It really was as I had learned along the way "the work of the people." In the liturgy there is nuance. In the liturgy we experience the rhythms of life, we participate in the sacramental mysteries, we sing the music and the melodies of our ancestors. The liturgy carries us, its fluidity the river of life: "Now the feast and celebration, all of creation sings for joy . . ."[1] In the dignity and reverence and beauty of the liturgy, there is a sense of the numinous. As an adult I know it is all of these and more.

In the liturgy, we rehearse these rhythms: birth and life and death, joy and sorrow, despair and hope. In the act of worship, we are practicing those rhythms, helping bear the reign of God into the world, colonizing heaven and making heaven—here, now. The liturgy is rehearsal, a lens for seeing and tasting and smelling— taste and see the goodness of God.

When I grow weary of happy, clappy church, as my Anglican friend describes her local parish, I return to the liturgy and the timeless stories of God's overwhelming love and saving acts. When I hear yet another sordid or depressing report about the church, its clergy, or its layers of institutional quicksand, I return to the liturgy where I find the brokenness somehow redeemed and reclaimed.

The liturgy is sacramental. It's a way for us to be formed into Christ's own body, a way to bear Christ to the world. It helps us understand the many meanings of the sacred. The liturgy celebrates God's presence in the most ordinary human things: birth and

---

1. Haugen, "Now the Feast."

death, the bonds of love between parents and children, marriage, a
healing touch, a shared meal. Benedictions all.

In liturgy, the light of God surrounds us, the love of God en-
folds us, the power of God protects us, and the presence of God
watches over us. Wherever we are, God is.

REFLECTION

Liturgy is a way for us to be formed into Christ's own body, a way
to bear Christ to the world.

* How is liturgy sacramental for you?

* What does it mean that liturgy is the work of the people?

* How does liturgy help reveal God?

* What keeps liturgy fresh, life-giving?

* How does liturgy become a benediction?

10

Apple Trees

In the raw cold of February and far from the gentle climate of my childhood, I begin to look for signs of spring, a benediction of hope. The apple tree outside my window looks dead, one last brown and rotted apple frozen and hanging precariously from a limb. There are no pussy willows, no green shoots of forsythia, no swollen buds of red rhubarb, no green spears of the first daffodils showing themselves. But as I look at the apple tree, I remember the day of my daughter Anne's confirmation several springs ago: apple blossoms everywhere, the trees thick with white and pink iridescent petals framing Annie and friends and family in the obligatory photos. I also remember two old and gnarled apple trees that framed the front of my grandparents' home. Each year as summer arrived we'd make daily trips to my grandmother's potting shed, an old sagging lean-to where we'd find a rusty iron rake for reaching the very biggest and fattest apples in those two trees.

May apple blossoms and warm, ripened, midsummer fruit are a far cry from the brown deadness of February. By March with some luck, I may find the beginnings of fine green crocus fronds buried beneath last fall's leaves. My obsession with possibilities begins in earnest in April when hope—nearly spent from the long

Midwestern winter—rises out of melting snow and winter's grit. But it will be May in Minnesota before spring really comes, when at long last tulips will lead the way into summer, their brilliant colors vibrating against the pale and washed-out canvas of a late spring.

In my garden book last year, I wrote "best arrangement yet" for the pattern of perennials, annuals, and vegetables I'd planted the previous spring. Then there is a list of what to try next year, what will come closer to those glorious pictures in my mind of my grandmother's garden, the carefully tended rose beds of old Aunt Katy, and the photographs in *Better Homes and Gardens*. The possibilities are infinite. Lavender. Delphinium. Hydrangea. If I choose the right varieties, we—the garden and I—may come a bit closer to that paragon of people who plant, the English and their magnificent gardens. This year I will shape a meandering path of old bricks. This year I will conquer the weeds. This year the flowers will be massive, dripping with color, large and small clumps of blue and red and yellow, short varieties at the front and in the back, tall willowy, delicate bunches of cleome and cosmos and oriental poppies swaying in the warm winds of summer.

Beneath the dead brown fronds of iris and the rotting leaves of fall, a frozen earth holds life, mystery. The words and melody of the dour Advent hymn "In the Bleak Midwinter" have only just gone out of my head. I am still remembering earth as hard as iron, water like a stone. William James' words of comfort to a down-cast friend come back to me: "Remember when old December's darkness is everywhere about you, that the world is really in every minutest point as full of life as in the most joyous morning you ever lived through; remember that the sun is whanging down, and the waves dancing, and the gulls skimming down at the mouth of the Amazon, for instance, as freshly as in the first morning of creation."[1]

A frozen apple dangles from a lifeless tree. Hidden now in February, new life will come again. And like Martin Luther, even

---

1. William James, in a letter to Thomas Ward, 1968.

if I knew that tomorrow the world would go to pieces, I would still plant my apple tree, a benediction in the cold of February.

REFLECTION

Even if knew that tomorrow the world would go to pieces, I would still plant my apple tree.

* When do you feel God's absence?

* In what ways can desolation or discouragement become holy ground, even a benediction?

* How do the cycles of the seasons affect you, comfort you, disturb you?

11

Waiting

The results of all the tests weren't as clear as we'd hoped—no tumor, no mass, a possible infection. The earlier removal of a fast-growing tumor was followed by weeks of radiation. Visits to doctors too numerous to list followed and through it all, my octogenarian father endured persistent pain and loss of energy, then loss of control of the left side of his face. Medications for controlling pain distorted reality, interacting with each other in negative and frightening ways. The *joie de vivre* that always had characterized my father's view of the world now seemed buried beneath a fragile scaffolding of pain management, interrupted sleep, and constant awareness that one's body has been invaded by dreaded cancer.

Like so many others, we wait. When will the economy begin to turn around? My child's disability will accompany us throughout his entire life—how will we cope? We've been excluded from full participation in the church for such a long time—how much longer must we wait? Our plan was to have children—we dreamed of a large family—but our hopes have been dashed again and again. Will the body of a much-loved husband, son, brother, friend buried in the rubble and ruins of Haiti be found? And how will we heal from such loss and sorrow?

Will new discoveries really make a difference for the millions of us who worry about loss of memory and Alzheimer's disease? When will the pain of losing a spouse begin to loosen its tenacious, crippling grip on a bereft widow whose life no longer seems worth living? Will the stem cells transplanted in a body ravaged by disease begin to grow and multiply, rebuilding a destroyed immune system and promising new life for at least a little longer?

For months we waited with patience, hoping our beloved father would be spared the suffering of cancer. Physically strong and always energetic, Dad's enthusiasm and passion for life were matched by deep faith. He left his first love of fisheries and the sea to become, of all things, a pastor. His encounter with grace and a loving God led him to seminary and parish ministry, the last place he ever dreamed of as his life's work. In retirement, he continued building boats hoping one day to sail them with children and grandchildren. But the cancer that had stalked him for months, perhaps years, returned and now we waited.

Waiting—sometimes without patience, sometimes without hope—is a fact of life. Children wait impatiently for birthdays, their little fingers awkwardly marking the years—one, two, three— so eager to grow up, to be big. We wait for peace in the Middle East, for water in dry and parched places around the world where drought seems never ending. We wait for acceptance into university or graduate school and then for jobs, spouses and partners, a family. And all along the way, we wait for God to reveal a holy presence, a palpable sense of the sacred in our everyday living and in our everyday dying.

In the summer of my father's eighty-fifth birthday, we waited with fragile hope knowing the waiting could not go on much longer. Finally at Christmastime as we held vigil at his bedside, the waiting was over and he breathed one last soundless breath. It was a benediction, a mysterious calm and ready sense that there is nothing—not death, not life, not things present and not things to come—that can separate us from God's love.

REFLECTION

Waiting with patience and hope, sometimes without patience, without hope, is a fact of life.

* For what do you wait and hope?
* What does it mean for you to wait for God to reveal who and what God is?
* How is waiting sometimes a benediction, a blessing?
* Why is it so difficult?

12

Real Life

D^{*ear Margit,*}
It's Thursday, almost the end of another long January, and I am thinking of you as you finish the last of the chemo treatments in preparation for the coming of February and what I imagine to be among the biggest challenges of your life, stem cell transplant. I think of this transplant like a miracle discovery (which I think it probably is) for planting healthy cells and allowing your body the chance to rebuild and regenerate. Reading your description of the process is overwhelming and I carry you in my heart every day, only able in the smallest of ways to imagine what you must be going through as you continue to do business with this dread disease I can barely pronounce.

With you in my heart, I sat today in the warm sunshine of our cabin's south facing windows to read a little tome about Celtic spirituality. I wasn't alone. The book in my lap had belonged to our mutual friend, Judy, whose death from breast cancer ten years ago was another real life journey. Looking over my shoulder as I read were two others with whom we've shared real life and circles of friendship.

The connection was good in and of itself but it went further. I'd only just read several saved notes from Arabella written during the last months of her life and I was trying to get hold of something that would give more direction to my own writing project. And, of course, I was thinking about you and all that you are facing.

So in the spirit of our covenant group and in the voices that continue to speak even though it may be through passed-along books or notes written and saved or poignant memories of life together while trying to make sense of real life and our place in it, I'm sharing a little of a chapter from Deborah Cronin's Holy Ground called "The Encircling Presence."

> Stand in a place that is holy ground to you. Extend your hand before you and point your index finger forward. As if on a pivot, turn, using your finger to draw a circle around yourself. You have just performed the Caim, "the Encircling." The Caim is a Celtic Christian acknowledgement of the presence of God, reminding us of the protection from danger and evil that God offers to each of us. It is not performing the Caim itself that provides shelter—God's presence is already with us. The Caim simply reminds us of this holy reality. The following prayer reflects the Celtic Christian understanding of the Caim.
>
> Circle me O God, keep hope within, despair without.
> Circle me O God, keep peace within, keep turmoil out.
> Circle me O God, keep calm within, keep storms without.
> Circle me O God, keep strength within, keep weakness out.[1]

Reading these words today, I hear the voices of each of us and I imagine drawing the circle and performing the Caim—making our claim for God's presence— encircling you with our love and care. You truly are surrounded by a great cloud—and even more by a loving and healing God. Real life. Real God.

Love, Julie

The Source of all life is our daily life and breath. This mysterious God who is gracious and generous beyond our wildest imagining continues to create and sustain a universe too big to comprehend. And at the same time, God walks the hills and valleys with each of us, dwelling within us and in every living thing.

---

1. Cronin, *Holy Ground*, 101–2.

God's spirit and presence—God's benediction—is woven into the everyday fabric of real life, rough cloth and smooth. No matter what befalls us, nothing can separate us from a God who comes to us in real life, in one another, in word and water, wine and bread. Real life is holy ground, marked and blessed by the presence and promises of God.

REFLECTION

God's spirit and presence—God's benediction—is woven into the everyday fabric of real life.

* Where is a place of holy ground for you?
* Describe how it feels to be in this place.
* What does it mean to you that the Source of all life is our daily life and breath?
* When have you felt encircled by the presence of God?

13

Practicing Resurrection

Pondering resurrection and rebirth has occupied Christians for centuries. Whatever our reasons for contemplating resurrection, rebirth is a primary theme in Christianity, taking its place at the head of the line for interpreting the power of God's saving acts.

All of us who experience the unfolding drama of Lent each year understand the centrality of Easter and resurrection. As the last dark hours of the three days come to a close, a massive door— not unlike the stone at the empty tomb—opens for Christians around the world: "Christ has risen! Alleluia! He is risen indeed. Alleluia!" Bells ring, light floods into once-dimmed sanctuaries, music reverberates and trumpets announce a new reality: death has been defeated. Christ lives!

In the northern hemisphere, the season of spring accompanies the Easter resurrection story and heralds new life in its own way. The stark brown barrenness of winter is transformed by the warming of the sun and the lengthening of days. New life erupts in shoots of swollen buds, blossoming trees, and the greening of the earth. What once seemed dead and lifeless is now vibrant again, full of hope and promise. Resurrection, rebirth, new life— ancient rituals reenacted in every time and place.

But resurrection—rebirth—is not limited to Easter's fanfare or the alchemy of spring. All who struggle with addictions or mental health issues know resurrection as a daily effort to keep enemies at bay. None of us is immune from dreaded medical diagnoses, dashed hopes and disappointments, worry about old age and depleted resources, anxiety for a world that often seems on the verge of self-destruction. When racism and systemic injustice erase dignity and hope to create their own tombs of death, one can hear the longing for resurrection in the desperate cries of people hanging onto life by a thread. All of us inhabit tombs of death and all of us long for rebirth, for resurrection.

Resurrection is restoration of life and hope in all the places where death and hopelessness once held sway. For a community in anguish over another tragic and irrational shooting, resurrection is shared heartbreak together with determined efforts to stop senseless acts of violence. A hospital in Jerusalem practices resurrection by providing medical care and tenacious hope in the face of unbelievable suffering and injustice. A group of miners buried thousands of feet below the surface of the earth experiences resurrection in their mutual vulnerability and the work of skilled technicians who finally free them from their tomb of death—a literal rebirth. For refugees consumed by the horrors of war and fleeing in desperation for their lives, resurrection is the fragile, complicated hope of new life in a new land together with the people who open their own doors to provide food and shelter.

Resurrection is the very essence of the nature of God, a call to life and a daily invitation to live with hope, mercy, love. Practicing resurrection is hard work, perhaps especially for ourselves but particularly for the broken world all around us. Pope Francis practices resurrection when he reminds us to "see the faces" and then embraces the weakest and most vulnerable in actions of affirmation and hope, mercy and grace.

Resurrection happens at the local homeless shelter where food is shared and beds offered. It's a loving touch, a helping hand, a compassionate voice. Resurrection includes acts of reassurance, words of recognition and encouragement, pots of soup and loaves of bread, extra blankets and open doors. We practice resurrection when we seek out a neighbor whose job has just been eliminated, walk with a friend whose marriage is on the rocks, and show our own vulnerability and need for daily resurrection and rebirth.

Resurrection is noticing God in one another and in the immeasurable ways people care for one another and for the earth that is our home. The power of resurrection is in us as we share the unutterable love of God and God's unconditional, sustaining mercy.

We are made in God's image. God lives in us. *We* are loved beyond our furthest imaginings. *We* bear God's resurrecting power to the world and to all we meet. May we practice resurrection as a benediction, showing God's lavish love and mercy as the very heart of what it means to be human.

REFLECTION

Resurrection is a call to life, a daily invitation to live with hope and mercy and love.

* What are some ways you experience rebirth in nature?
* Have you thought before about resurrection as a metaphor for all the ways God offers rebirth and new life?
* Why do you think we limit or literalize our understandings of resurrection life?
* Share an example of resurrection that you've experienced.

14

Helpers

Making sense of suffering and adversity is never easy. An unrelenting litany of natural disasters, conflict and warfare around the world, frightening medical diagnoses, challenging financial worries, or family dysfunction of one sort or another seem to be common ground for all of us. Our access to technology means that we experience all these things sooner, in more detail, and more graphically than ever before. Social media and the millions of exchanges it provides adds another layer of overload until finally, we simply shut down unable to absorb any more information, unable to feel so much pain, so much suffering.

Today as I write, the headlines and lead stories tell of another devastating earthquake. Thousands of people have been buried beneath the rubble, thousands are homeless. Words and pictures don't begin to capture such horrific grief and suffering. In the Middle East, tribal and factional warfare continues to maim and rob innocent people of basic human rights. Religious extremism is rampant. In the United States, racial tension has reached another high with widespread fear and anger fueling riots and justifying mayhem. The richest country in the world, our own, seems unable to stem the disparity between rich and poor and the widening chasm between these two extremes threatens our democracy.

As much as we may want to close our eyes and plug our ears, it isn't an option of course. We are part of this litany, part of the chaos, part of the hope. And even as the need for mutuality and action grows, it's clear that the appalling suffering of so many will not be obliterated by equal examples of self-sacrifice, generosity, or selfless giving. Still, we know the power of caring for one another and perhaps no one illustrated it any better than Fred Rogers, the iconic children's television personality.

"Look at the helpers, always look for the helpers," was the mantra bestowed by his mother on Mr. Rogers. Whenever disasters struck or the traumas of everyday life, large and small, seemed too much, Fred Rogers's mother would remind him again and again, "Look for the helpers." And in his warm and engaging way, Mr. Rogers helped children (and adults) navigate the stormy waters of being human by reminding them of their uniqueness and inviting them to notice the helpers. His calm and reassuring presence in the face of fear or loss or any other ordeal made fear and tragedy more manageable.

Noticing the helpers is a way of seeing hope. Noticing the helpers is a way of seeing how to make a difference. As we walk together in a world often overwhelmed with sorrow and suffering, noticing the helpers makes us more human by making helpers of each of us. The same mantra may not help make *sense* of suffering and hardship but it gives us another lens for paying attention and acting and it saves us from despair and cynicism.

Today as I lament the brokenness of so much of life, I re-member the helpers: relief agencies on the ground in Nepal and Iran and Haiti, journalists who risk their lives to shed light on the plight of women and children in countries ravaged by perpetual conflict and war, clergy who walk hand in hand to protest violence and promote peaceful negotiation, food kitchens and community shelters where hungry people are fed and given a place to sleep, political and religious leaders who act to address injustice and challenge the status quo, parents and teachers and mentors and community organizers. These helpers embody what it means to be human. They show us the face of Christ because they are willing to risk life, even lose life, for the sake of others.

These helpers are us, benedictions and blessings that don't eliminate sorrow or fear but rather show love and humanity in the face of despair and suffering. In the spirit of Christ, we bring hope in the midst of despair, comfort in hardship, blessing in adversity. As helpers—such a simple word, such a high calling—we become the hands and face of Christ in all the places where suffering and sorrow weigh us down.

REFLECTION

Today as I lament the brokenness of so much of life, I remember the helpers . . .

* In the face of suffering and adversity, what saves you from despair and cynicism?

* How do you understand hope?

* Does Mr. Rogers's image of the helpers resonate for you? Why or why not?

* What does it mean to you to be the hands and face of Christ?

15

God Is Here

There are many versions of the story I retell here. Because it speaks eloquently about a longing we all share for new life and vitality or perhaps because it can be translated for any time and place, the meaning of the mythical story continues to resonate as a timeless benediction.[1]

In an isolated monastery in a far-off place, the monks and their abbot had lived together a very long time. They were old, set in their ways, fearful and crotchety. No one new came to the monastery any longer and the handful of tired monks bickered. They were tired, afraid, and critical of one another. Their small community clearly was on the brink of dying. One day the abbot sensed that a wise rabbi had come to a small hermitage in the forest near the monastery. At the urging of his fellow monks, he decided to make a visit to the rabbi. Perhaps this wise rabbi would be able to help them save their dying community?

So the abbot set off through the forest and at last came to a hut where the rabbi was staying. He welcomed the abbot,

---

1. This story, likely a myth, appears in many places. The source of the version here is obscure. I listened to it on the video *The Rabbi's Gift*, from Franciscan Communications. It also appears in the prologue of *The Different Drum*, by M. Scott Peck (1987).

embracing him sorrowfully and they sat together for a long time in silence. Both seemed to know intuitively the sadness of dying communities. After some time, they began to speak to one another, acknowledging the losses both in the monastery and in the synagogue where the rabbi said few came any longer to pray and learn. After a lengthy exchange, the abbot prepared to leave but at the door, he turned to the rabbi to ask a hard question. "We are dying," he said bluntly. "The spirit has gone out of our people. Where is the Messiah?" Upon which the rabbi looked thoughtfully at the old abbot and responded quietly, "The Messiah is in your midst. The Messiah is one of you."

And with this enigmatic message, the abbot returned to the monastery to explain to his monks the rabbi's strange words. "Well, what did the rabbi say?" they asked. As the abbot told the monks the strange thing the rabbi had said, they all began to look at one another. "Surely the abbot is not the Messiah but if anyone comes close, he'd be the one," and "Brother Thomas? He has some Christlike ways but he's often surly—it couldn't be him," and "Brother Eldred is quiet and thoughtful but he loses his temper and can be so obnoxious," and "Brother Philip is a total nobody, passive, boring. But on the other hand, he often helps when no one else will . . . the rabbi couldn't have meant him, could he?" And finally, each said to himself, "The rabbi surely couldn't have meant me, could he?"

Then out of awkward curiosity and an uneasy sense that the Messiah might be one of them, they began to treat each other differently. And on the entirely ludicrous chance—could it really be?—that the Messiah might be living in their very midst, they began to look differently at themselves, their community, the world. A deeply profound and palpable spirit of respect and kindness began slowly to transform bitterness and fear, the thick cloud of despair lifting and vanishing. After some time had passed, people began to come back to the monastery. Younger monks were interested in joining the community and people in outlying areas were drawn to its doors. Seeing Christ in their midst, the monastery once again became a center of hope and light, mercy and grace.

God's unmistakable presence, a benediction, was evident in a tangible spirit of joy and new life.

The living God is in *our* midst, making God's home among us. God's kingdom *is* here in this place. When we bear Christ to one another, treating each other and the world we share with compassion and dignity, loving relationships flourish. No one is left out, excluded, or uncared for. May we see Christ in each other, in the rich and the poor, the despised and the esteemed. And may the church, our homes, and the communities we're all part of reflect the transforming presence of Christ. God is here!

REFLECTION

The living God is in our midst, making God's home among us.

*   Saint Augustine wrote, "God was within and we mistakenly sought him without." How do you understand *"God within"*?

*   What are some noticeable characteristics of communities or churches that seem to thrive and flourish?

*   In what other realms do you experience this spirit of respect and dignity?

16

Wisdom Stories

Making sense of belief and faith is a lifelong journey. In our search to find ever more spacious meanings for God, we discover again and again that God is elusive and indescribable, a moving target for our neat definitions. Now almost two decades into a new century, many once acceptable definitions or ways of speaking about God's presence no longer fit. As the church experiences uncertainty and change—perhaps even a radical shift in the ways it interprets Christian life and faith—we founder as well for new ways of understanding God.

The biblical stories are at the heart of our identity as Christians. By connecting us to the creeds, songs, sagas, and dramas of other searchers, they remind us that we are not unique in our striving to know and be known by God. Passed from generation to generation, the stories of the Bible are benedictions to be interpreted and reinterpreted, accompanying us in our lifelong seeking of God's face.

In another reflection, I recount the experience of the Vigil of Easter, when Christians come together to recall God's activity down through the ages. Listening on Easter Eve to one vividly told story after another—creation, flood, covenants made, covenants broken, captivity and deliverance, bones taking on flesh, rascals and renegades being rescued from mess after mess—there emerges an intensely compelling picture of a loving and gracious God.

As each salvation story is told or enacted, God is revealed as the source of all life, the creator of the universe, the one who brings life out of death, who makes all things new, who saves and resurrects time and time again. Every story seems to lead to resurrection and new life. The church, the body of Christ, must be a place of living stories where, if we pay attention, we discover ourselves in an ongoing drama of human and divine history. Weekly worship invites us into these stories of wisdom to discover a new way of being in the world. Engagement with Scripture shows us all kinds of occasions when others have wrestled with who and what God is and with what it means to be human.

Centuries of telling and retelling, interpreting and reinterpreting the biblical stories help convey the deep wisdom found in Scripture. Multilayered biblical narratives free us from self-absorption by pointing us away from ourselves toward others and our creator God, connecting us to other times and places. Their themes are both simple and profound—God's overwhelming love for humankind and God's admonishment to love the neighbor as oneself—words of grace that echo across the centuries.

In his book *The Gates of the Forest*, writer and Holocaust survivor Elie Wiesel says that God made us because God loves stories. I like to think that God chose stories as a way of imparting wisdom. They help us understand a God who lives among us now, here in this place. I imagine the stories of Scripture as signs and symbols, a lens for conveying the wisdom of God. I think of them as benedictions, prayers, blessings for sustaining us along life's journey.

It's challenging—sometimes even unnerving—finding roomier and more spacious words and images for God. An all-too-human church and sometimes worn-to-death ways of interpreting the stories of Scripture can sap our ability to think about questions of faith and belief, doubt and unbelief. Sometimes they obscure the very resurrection life we crave. But inherited belief and unexamined faith seem somehow empty.

The stories of Scripture are wisdom stories—benedictions that ring true to help us make sense of ourselves and the world we inhabit. Their layers of meaning have the power to change us, to transfix and transform, assault and convict, reveal and confuse. They show us the multifaceted face of God in all the complexities of being human in our time and throughout human history. Wresting new meaning from our definitions of God and from the stories of Scripture is lifelong and life-giving.

REFLECTION

The stories of Scripture . . . are wisdom stories—benedictions that ring true to help us make sense of ourselves and the world we inhabit.

* In what ways do you wrestle with questions of faith, of belief?
* Which stories of Scripture are especially revealing or meaningful for you?
* Which stories seem confusing or too difficult to unravel?
* Why do we often feel uncomfortable about our search for new ways of understanding God?
* How might we encourage one another to speak about ways of wrestling with our definitions and interpretations of God?

17

Music

Landing in Tel Aviv, anxious, perhaps even a little wary, a group of sixty musicians from an American college begin their spring tour in the Holy Land. Their arrival is a mix of excitement and curiosity as they wait for passport checks, luggage, and mountains of carefully crated instruments. They're here to experience daily life in a complicated part of the Middle East and they're here to share their love of music by performing and making music with young Palestinian musicians.

In Bethlehem and Jerusalem, in Ibillin and the Galilee, endless hours of practice precede each performance and become the common ground for learning to know one another. Between rehearsals and over shared meals, camaraderie happens and bonds of understanding are formed and become part of the poignancy of the music. On the Mount of Olives, their instruments in tow, the students bring music to the wards of Augusta Victoria Hospital, playing in small chamber groups for patients and staff. In Ramallah the day after a confrontation in which two teenagers are shot and killed, these American and Palestinian musicians come together in their grief to dedicate a somber and melancholy concert to the memories of the two young men. That evening the packed concert hall is heavy with the weight of death and the music becomes a haunting lament as well as a robust declaration, a benediction of solidarity in the face of so much grief and loss.

In another place far from the Middle East, we travel west making our way across the wintery plains of the Montana prairie, watching for the first jagged peaks of the Rocky Mountains on the far edge of the horizon. Expectations of Christmas and family and time together color the long journey but the music is what I remember best.

With the mountains finally in full view and an iPod playing at full volume, the music of English composer John Rutter reverberates around us, transporting us beyond the place and beyond the time. "For the beauty of the earth, for the beauty of the skies, for the love which from our birth, over and around us lies, Lord of all, to thee we raise, this our joyful hymn of praise." Over and over again, Rutter's lyrical arrangement accompanies us along a winding highway connecting the plains to the massive snow-covered peaks of the Rocky Mountains.

Traveling in the company of choirs and composers, of orchestras and musicians, sacred music and texts, people seen and unseen, music is more than music. It washes over us and carries us along, transforming ordinary experiences into something extraordinary and life-changing. It's another of the ways we experience the mystery of God's sacred presence. "For the beauty of each hour, of the day and of the night, hill and vale, and tree and flower, sun and moon and stars of light . . . for the joy of human love, brother, sister, parent, child, friends on earth, and friends above . . . "[1]

I remember, too, a garish sanctuary filled with too much Christmas and a family mourning the long and difficult dying of a loved one. I remember the music that cradled and supported us, filling aching hearts and a troubled family with a palpable sense of God's presence and peace. "God is my shepherd, so nothing shall I want . . . gently you raise me and heal my weary soul . . . you have set me a banquet of love . . . Shepherd me, O God, beyond my

---

1. Pierpoint, "For the Beauty of the Earth."

wants, beyond my fears, from death into life"—the words and the music a benediction for making sense of loss and grief.[2]

A few years earlier, we stood in a college chapel on a hot September afternoon, its cavernous space punctuated by shafts of light, tense with the emotions of children and their parents ready and not ready for this next stage of life. Music reverberated across this sacred space, holding all of us together, wrapping itself around our hearts. "Go my children, with my blessing, never alone. Waking, sleeping, I am with you, you are my own. In my love's baptismal river, I have made you mine forever, Go my children, with my blessing, you are my own."[3]

Music is so much more than beautiful words and unforgettable melodies. Music is transcendent, universal, a common language through which we express joy and sorrow and everything in between. Music transports us, often taking us places we never intended to go, a medium for our deepest emotions, a bottomless well from which to draw. It binds us together and helps us express what words cannot convey. It helps us bear the dread of a final farewell, an unexpected loss, inexplicable joy, another passage.

Music has the power to bring us together in a common longing for the common good. It makes us more than we were before as it accompanies us along life's way. And yes, music can change the world. Visit with a group of young musicians whose music became a benediction, holy ground in a war-torn land whose people long for true holiness, for beauty and for peace.

REFLECTION

Part of the poignancy of music is its ability to form bonds of understanding, to unite us in our common humanity.

* In what ways does music function as a benediction for you?

* What are some ways you experience music as holy ground, a way to express joy, sorrow, another way of seeing God?

2. Haugen, "Shepherd Me, O God."
3. Vajda, "Go, My Children, with My Blessing."

* What liturgies, hymns or songs are important for you? Can you sing them from memory?

18

Tables

Who can resist a beautifully illustrated cookbook or a flat of freshly picked ripe raspberries or a fabulous display of garden produce at a farmer's market in the peak of summer? Food is so much more than daily sustenance and tables are so much more than places to gather for eating together.

It isn't just the beauty of a well-tended table, carefully set with cloth and candle, flower and fruit. Neither is it only the creative satisfaction and culinary delight over preparing beautiful food to grace the table. Nor is it entirely the rich collection of memories shaped and shared around the many tables of our lives. It's all these things and so much more.

Our first table was a wedding gift. To that table, we brought memories of life together around earlier tables in our lives—farm tables laden with food at harvest time; an old and weathered picnic table where we cracked crab and feasted on fish on the island where I grew up; kitchen tables, coffee tables, communion tables.

Around these many tables, we heard family stories and re-lived family memories. Sometimes there were heated debates and arguments. Always there were prayers of thanks and acknowledgement that the food, the bonds of belonging, and the rituals were gifts from a generous and gracious God. We knew the table to be sacred space, holy ground, a benediction. We knew that food and drink were not only for us but to be shared and celebrated with friends, with strangers, with outsiders, and most of all with those who were hungry. Along the way, we learned that we ourselves were to be food and drink for one another.

Food and feasting are major biblical themes and the table is about holy hospitality. It's a welcome place, a threshold inviting us to be part of something larger than ourselves. In the tents of our Old Testament ancestors, guests at the table were safe from the attack of enemies—"You prepare a table before me in the presence of my enemies; you anoint my head with oil; my cup overflows." Hospitality meant being welcomed and protected by a loving God.

God spreads a banquet at the many tables of our lives. God invites us to welcome one another, to be God's hands, to be little Christ's, to bear one another's burdens. Our tables should be places for welcoming strangers, outsiders, people with whom we might disagree, those who may make us uncomfortable or be very different from familiar friends and family. In this way, our tables reflect God's table, a place of welcome for all. At God's table and at our tables, we share a common longing for meaning and for leading lives that matter. These are tables where the face of God is revealed to us, where no one is excluded, where all are forgiven, fed, and welcomed. These are the tables where we experience the mystery of the source of life.

The tables of our lives come in all shapes and sizes and they convey so much more than fine food, important conversations, places for gathering. Tables are for making time for one another, for being present, for paying attention. God is here! God meets us at these sacred tables—inviting us to be food and drink for one another, inviting us to welcome the stranger and feed the hungry, welcoming us to be part of the body of Christ. Holy hospitality is God's gift, the welcome table we're all invited to share. Taste and see the goodness of God!

REFLECTION

We knew the table to be sacred space, holy ground, a benediction.

* How might the tables of our lives help reveal the mystery of God?

* What do you do to make table life important?

* How are the tables of everyday life like the table of the Lord?

* What does it mean to you to be food and drink for one another?

19

More!

Achieving the good life seems to be the text behind the text in much of American life and culture. If advertising is any measure, that's surely the case. Bigger, shinier, better, *more!* Television and social media convey an unrelenting stream of temptations, a barrage of promotions promising cures for our ailments, a better way of life, and more stuff than any of us want or need. Recessions come and go and even in times of economic downturn, we continue to fill omnipresent storage units with the excess *more* that no longer fits into our jam-packed homes. Our sense of entitlement, confidence, good fortune, and access to *more* runs deep and strong.

While optimism seems inherent in the American spirit, this expectation of *more* is the defining characteristic of the good life. More money. More stuff. More time. More meaning. More connections. More life. In the culture of relative affluence and comfort that most of us inhabit, there's a constant drumbeat encouraging us to seek *more*. And coming up with a long list of over-the-top luxuries emblematic of first world affluence and comfort—the *more* of our culture—would not be hard for us.

The *more* of living mindfully, paying attention to benedictions that convey God's grace and mercy is a kind of *more* wholly different from the drum beat of a consumer-driven culture. At every turn, the *more* of Christianity points to sacrifice, to emptying, to feeding, to giving one's life away. The *More* of Christmas comes to us as a helpless child, a lowly baby born in a manger stall to a poor peasant woman. The *More* of Lent and Easter empties himself, suffers and dies, showing us more love, more forgiveness, more acceptance, more peace, more justice. The *more* of Lent and Easter is what Christians call the resurrection life—more life, less death—truly the good life.

What keeps many connected to the church is its counter-cultural voice that will not let us succumb to our insatiable appetite for *more*. The *more* to be found in Christianity is the way it calls us away from self-preoccupation to life together, life lived with others and for others. The compelling *more* of Christian life is the sacrificial love of Christ, *more* love and *more* mercy than we can fathom.

The *more* many look for in the church is its unrelenting willingness to challenge our sense of comfort and entitlement. And truth to tell, the *more* many long for is quite likely the *more* our culture seeks as well: a deeper sense of meaning and purpose; connectedness among families and friends, communities and nations; the will to make the world a place of peace and justice—all signs, benedictions, that the *More* we call God is woven into the life we all share.

The *More* that truly characterizes the good life, a benediction life, is that which brings life out of death, healing out of suffering, joy out of sorrow. The *More* of benediction life is a gracious and loving God found in the people we meet and the world we've been given to care for and tend. Curbing our hunger for *more* helps us better know the *More* who has created and redeemed us, set us free, invited us to be part of the *More* that makes life worth living.

Holy and gracious God, you are the *More* we long for, the essence of the good life. Pour out a benediction on our insatiable appetites. Open our eyes, open our hearts, open our lives so that we might reflect the *More* that brings life out of death, healing out of suffering, joy out of sorrow. Holy and gracious God, what *more* do we need?

REFLECTION

Curbing our hunger for *more* helps us better know the *More* who creates and redeems us, sets us free, invites us to be part of the *More* that makes life worth living.

* What are some ways we might learn to curb or limit our ever-present hunger for *more*?

* Who do you know who seems to live simply, even sacrificially?

* Discuss how our appetites for *more* may be about a longing for *More*.

* How might *More* explain something of the mystery of God?

20

Learning to Be *We*

As the grains of wheat, once scattered on the hill, were gathered into one to become our bread; so may all your people, from all the ends of earth, be gathered into one in you.[1]

Fields of sun-ripened wheat, the grains ground to the powdery softness of sifted flour, yeast that comes alive in a sticky ball of kneaded dough, a crusty loaf of freshly baked bread . . . And this melding of ordinary things an example—a picture of the people of God scattered across every time and every place, gathered into one to become bread. Bread for the world, the bread of life, the body of Christ called to feed the world, to *be* Christ's body in the world. Such remarkable images!

Us! We are the body of Christ. We share the holy meal becoming what we eat and drink, Christ's own body blessed and broken for the life of the world. This is why we receive the bread and wine of the Eucharist with an amen!—to acknowledge what we are. Too often, this body of Christ we struggle to describe looks more like a mix of oil and water. Forget the yeast. Forget the coming together.

---

1. Haugen, "As the Grains of Wheat."

We cling to individualism, to denominational loyalties, to nation-alism and our well-articulated corners on the truth. It's easy to be skeptical about what it means to be the body of Christ. Caring about unity, the common good, neighborliness, the brokenness of our own lives and the brokenness of our world is a big order.

Our culture is proud of making its own way. We're fiercely protective of individual rights, adamant about each person's claim to life, liberty, and the pursuit of happiness. We value our indepen-dence even when it comes at the expense of others. And while we may be connected to larger communities—church, neighborhood groups, civic organizations, even the Internet and web connec-tions and networks—it's easy for us to think individually, to focus on *me* rather than *we*.

Perhaps there is no more important challenge to twenty-first-century Christians than learning to think communally and globally, working to live together as the body of Christ. African cultures have a word for this: *Ubuntu*. It means I am because we are. It means we are because Christ is. It means we do life together! *Ubuntu* is a benediction, a way of understanding that personal identity is integral to communal identity and that all identity comes from Christ.

To think communally means learning to be *we*, the body of Christ in all its diversity. It means putting aside our differences, be-coming food and drink for one another, caring about the common good, pointing the way to our common God. It means thinking of ourselves as the face of Christ, reflecting a God who loves the world and calls us to care for it and for one another in every way imaginable.

Learning to be *we* is what it means to be the body of Christ. In the words of liturgical language scholar Gail Ramshaw, "Prayer is not about the me who is, but about the us whom faith hopes we become." In our praying, in our life together, in our struggle to be Christ's body in the world, may we learn to be *we*.

> *One bread, one body, one Lord of all . . . One cup of bless-ing which we bless . . .*

And we, though many, throughout the earth . . . We are
one body in this one Lord.[2]

REFLECTION

Prayer is not about the me who is, but about the us whom faith hopes we become.

* Name some ways the concept of *Ubuntu* might be a benediction.

* How might it be possible to talk with people of other faith traditions, other religious groups, about the things we share in common?

* As we watch ongoing effects of religious extremism, global warming, racial tension, it seems more important than ever to learn to be *we*. What might be some ways to begin community or communal conversations?

2. Foley, "One Bread, One Body."

21

God Be with You

Perhaps more than any other benediction, the holy act of saying *God be with you* has been a lifelong gift. As my father endured the ravages of cancer in the last years of his life, he and I learned to communicate long distance between his home in the Pacific Northwest and mine in Minnesota. It wasn't easy. Dad was not comfortable talking about fear or worry or matters close to the heart. When I'd want to discuss the latest radiation treatment and its effects or the results of a recent PET scan or the many ways chemotherapy diminished my father's quality of life, he was deft at redirecting the conversation.

God be with you—a benediction we'd exchanged all our lives—took on new depth and new weight as words and expressions of concern had to be parsed more carefully. "God be with you," I'd say to my father as we concluded regular evening phone calls. And with worry evident in the tone of his still strong voice, he'd reply, "And also with you."

Two years ago in New York City, the too-short life of my friend Arabella was remembered and celebrated by friends and family who continue to grieve her death from pancreatic cancer. "God be with you, dear friend," I said to Arabella in the last phone call before she became so ill that we could no longer communicate. And in the many conversations we shared together over those last years of her life—in quiet places where we gathered to share stories of hope and laments of loss—always in my heart and often on my lips was the promise of *God be with you.*

The words were a gift from my mother. I don't remember when *God be with you* became a ritual in our family, a way of blessing one another. I don't think it was intentional and I know it wasn't some kind of cheap expression of "good luck" or a variation of "safe travels." My mother's very being was imbued with a sense of God being with us. Whether we were leaving for school in the morning, anticipating a dreaded exam, preparing for a challenging event or worried about life in general, Mom's grace to us was *God be with you.*

It bore no sense of what could sometimes seem pious or sentimental. It was plain and stark: God be with you. Not an invitation to God. More than a reminder to us. An acknowledgment: God is with you. God is with us. God is. All is well.

With my own children, it became our morning prayer as they left each day and we all went our separate ways. Now when we live long distances from each other, *God be with you* is often our farewell gift. I say it easily and feel it keenly. My spouse's reply is always, "And with you too." I know his deep faith and find comfort in sharing this benediction.

For as long as I can remember, *God be with you* has been an everyday prayer, a ritual acknowledgement of God's presence and grace. God be with you today, my dear family, as we continue to heal following the deaths of our parents. God be with you, dear Arabella, as you join the saints and leave so many of us feeling bereft of the joy you brought to our lives. God be with you, my beloved children. And God be with all of us, readers and writers and all whose lives continue to bear witness to the mystery of God's power and presence in everyday life.

REFLECTION

There are many ways to bless one another, many ways to pray.

* What blessing might you offer when greeting or saying good-bye to someone you love?

* Together with *God be with you*, practice making the sign of the cross, another form of benediction, when you wake in the morning or before going to sleep at night.

* If you have children, offer them the gift of *God be with you*.

* When words seem inadequate or even inappropriate, try offering *God be with you*.

* Notice the grace of benediction in the words, *God be with you*.

22

Singers of Life

Anthropologist and naturalist Loren Eiseley was an ardent observer of nature. Among the many stories he told is one of being awakened by a great ruckus in a forest where he was napping. To the horror of many other small birds in that wooded place, an enormous black raven had captured a small nestling and was preparing to make a meal of his squirming prey. As the small hawks watched in silence and fear, the forest became a morgue of anticipated death.

But in the last seconds before the little nestling died, one hawk and then another and another began to sing. The clear notes of their bird song carried across the wooded ravine until a great symphony of song shifted their attention from imminent death to the beauty of life. No longer were they afraid. No longer were they focused on death. They were singers of life whose symphony of sound acknowledged the goodness and the beauty of life even in the midst of death.[1]

Christians claim a God who brings life out of death. Like Mary whose life is turned upside down by an unmanageable God—a God who does wild and crazy things like making God

---

1. Raines, *Creative Brooding*, 36.

incarnate in Jesus—we too are asked to be vessels, God-carriers, Christ-bearers and yes, singers of life. Like Noah or Moses or Rahab or the widow of Zarephath, we have lots of reasons for not responding. But this generous and unrelenting God continues to shower us with gift upon gift, unmerited love and grace. Our response to the overwhelming love of God, the Singer of life, is to be singers of life ourselves.

We all know loss and fear, insecurity and vulnerability. We all experience disappointment and the darkness that is part of life. We're well-acquainted with grief and sorrow. But I am struck by the words and images painted by Loren Eiseley in the forest that day.

Rather than a cacophony of wailing or the emptiness of silence, harmonious song is raised even as the nestling loses its life. In the shadow of the hulking predator and the certainty of imminent death, the little hawks turn their heads away and look up, up into the forested cathedral surrounding the sorrowful scene. Shafts of light penetrate the darkness. Bird song echoes among the vast canopy of trees and forest and together the small hawks follow the lead of one, their song coming together in a benediction to affirm light and life even in the midst of death.

And so we sing. We sing our gratitude for each other, for the gift of life, for green and growing things, for the seasons that come and go in a never-ending cycle of beauty and change. We sing because we have voices for making the world a better place. We sing because we know that death does not have the last word and we sing knowing that our voices are joined to other voices, helping bear another's sorrows and sharing another's joy. Even in the midst of unbearable suffering, we sing our thanks for a church that courageously affirms Christ's commitment to the poor, the hungry, the outsider, and to those caught in all the downward spirals of death.

We sing in response to the Singer of life. As song-makers, life-givers, pain-bearers, we become co-creators with this God of life. We sing because God is here among us, in each other, in the sorrows and joys of life, in the broken places and in the darkness of death. We sing because the hulking bird of death doesn't have the last word. We sing because the darkness of the forest is penetrated by the light of Christ. We sing because the Light of Christ is a Singer of life.

REFLECTION

As song-makers, life-givers, pain-bearers, we become co-creators with the God of life.

* What does it mean to you to be a singer of life?
* How is this different from "making the best of things?"
* Who are some people you know who are singers of life?
* What makes them authentic?
* How is the God of life found in dark places?

23

Hunger and Thirst

January is a time of new beginnings. At the top of a fresh new
year, many of us like to chart out ways for living more intention-
ally. We want our lives to matter, to make a difference. Filled with
determination, we march into a new year with high expectations
and a long list of resolutions for bettering ourselves and the lives
of those around us.

Then just as our best intentions and dogged determination
begin to lag and reality sets in, the season of Lent appears. Strange
as it might seem, I long for this season of the church year. Perhaps
it's the relief from the weight and starry-eyed optimism of January's resolutions. Lent is a season of truth telling. It's no nonsense,
basic. Beginning with Ash Wednesday and that smudge of black,
gritty ash marking us with the sign of Christ and the starkly frank
words, "You are dust and to dust you shall return," we are carried,
eyes wide open, all the way through the despair of Holy Week and
finally into the heart of the Christian year, Easter and resurrection.

In the northern hemisphere, the dreary last days of winter
mark a forty-day journey in the spirit of those ancient ancestors
of ours, the Israelites. Wandering through deserts of our own, we
muddle along looking for meaning and purpose, talking, mulling,

and reflecting about our situation in life, the turmoil of the world, a culture that more often than not seems bent on destruction.

Eagerly wanting to make a difference, we put our heads down determined to work harder and harder to create lives that matter. We want to be successful. We want to make a difference. We want to help bring about the kingdom of God in all the places where we see a gaping need for new life and resurrection, for justice and peace. There is no end of worthy projects, legitimate goals, and authentic reasons for our goal-filled lives. And we want to do all these things here, now.

Listen with me to storyteller, John Shea:

> When the shadows were long and the days of sharing short, Jesus sent out his disciples without cloak or coin, possessing only his words like troubadours with a single song. They broke over Galilee like a summer storm, cleansing air and earth and leaving a fragrance as fresh as the time before the first scream. They returned with the step of soldiers.
>
> "We have broken the back of pain, pushed ignorance into the sea, and stomped sour grapes into wine," they said.
>
> Jesus said, "Come away with me and rest awhile, earth-shakers, mountain-movers, demon-killers, sin-stalkers." And Jesus pulled them away from the hordes of people to a deserted place where the disciples reclined on the green grass of Jesus' soul.
>
> "We have done great things," they said.
>
> Jesus said, "Your feet are dusty. I will wash them."
>
> "We will make a time of no hunger and no thirst," they said.
>
> Jesus replied, "People who would do away with hunger must themselves be hungry. Here is bread. People who would do away with thirst must themselves be thirsty. Here is wine."[1]

John Shea goes on to say that hunger and thirst are the invitations God places in us to God's banquet. Not "no hunger" but hunger fed. Not "no thirst" but thirst quenched. Not a time without needs but this time with needs met.

1. Shea, *Stories of Faith*, 163–64.

Shea isn't about closing our eyes and hearts to the deep needs of the world. But he reminds us to eat and remember! He reminds us that the earth we shake will swallow us and the mountains we move will crush us. Most of all, he reminds us that we too need to come away and rest awhile. He reminds us of our own need for the green grass of Jesus' soul. Hunger and thirst are holy ground.

REFLECTION

Hunger and thirst are the invitations God places in us to God's banquet.

* What does it mean to you that hunger and thirst are invitations to God's banquet?

* How can hunger and thirst be benedictions, holy ground?

* When do you feel hunger? Thirst?

24

Sunday Benedictions

Bear with me as I write this night, overwhelmed yet again by the news of the day, the week, the year—an unrelenting saga of heartbreak and tragedy delivered in the past via morning papers, radio, and the evening television news. I could well understand the counsel then from theologian Reinhold Niebuhr who advised his students always to read the newspaper in one hand with the Bible in the other, looking for context and matrix and the intersections of life and faith.

Today we're awash in information and nonstop news reporting from every corner of the world. It comes at us like a raging river in springtime threatening to drown us in its urgency and drama. I'm grateful for much of it. We need to see the faces of refugee families fleeing for their lives. We need to know and feel what it means to be caught in a natural disaster or a bloody coup or another senseless shooting. But it takes a toll. Just as too much junk food robs our bodies of vital nourishment, the effect of receiving and absorbing the 24-7 barrage of news reporting is an assault on our minds and souls as toxic as malnourished bodies.

So I write this night after a long week. The Middle East is a smoldering cauldron of fear and anger. Congress is in gridlock. It's the hurricane season and coastal towns are preparing for a hard hit. An acquaintance and his family lost their home in a fire a few months ago. A dear friend struggles with alcoholism and another with Parkinson's disease. This is life for all of us. We are in desperate need of healing oil and sheltering comfort—not as an escape from the world but as a way of being in the world.

Tomorrow is Sunday. After a long week, we will gather like hungry birds, weary of doing and making and being, ready to participate in this alternative way of being in the world. We come together to remember who we are, to lament and pray, hope and sing. Confessions are made, blessings are given, peace is offered, bread is broken, wine is poured, all are fed. Tomorrow we participate in the drama of a long history of news reporting chronicling times as complicated in some ways as our own. Tomorrow we will enact God's saving acts on our behalf knowing ourselves to be God's own healing oil and sheltering comfort.

Sunday, this day set apart for Sabbath rest, offers gifts of renewal, restoration, and resurrection. Balm for tired souls, yes. Healing oil and sheltering comfort, yes. But Sunday also calls us from despair and hopelessness to action. Sunday's benediction calls us to be bearers of benedictions, healers, comforters, the very hands and face of the Christ we worship. Sunday's blessing is time for balancing the sorrows that are part of everyday life with the joy that is at the heart of Christianity, time for remembering and time for being.

The spirit of God is present in each of us. We are God's dwelling place. We are God's home. Sunday invites us to stop. With the heartache and worry of the week's news still ringing in our ears and surrounded, even on Sunday, by the clamor of football games and news programs and social media all vying for our attention, Sunday asks of us a moment for silence. Sunday prompts us to remember, to taste and see, to walk with and act, to speak and to listen, to hear the still small voice inside each of us calling us to be benedictions for one another.

Go in peace. Serve God. Allow yourself to hear and absorb the suffering of the world. Be the face and hands of Christ in the places where you live. Use your voice and your resources to make a difference. Care for yourself and for sisters and brothers whose lives are a daily struggle for survival. Be grace, hope, joy, mercy. Help us, O God, to become healing oil and sheltering comfort for those in darkness and despair. Holy God, eternal spirit, earth-maker, pain-bearer, life-giver, help us bring life out of death.

REFLECTION

Go in peace. Serve God. Allow yourself to hear and absorb the suffering of the world. Be the face and hands of Christ in the places where you live.

* In what ways do Sundays serve as a benediction for you?

* If not, where do you find rest, renewal, resurrection?

* Describe some ways you've experienced healing oil or sheltering comfort.

* Is it possible to live the joy at the heart of Christianity in such a troubled world?

25

Doubt and Darkness

W*hen I was a child, I spoke like a child, I thought like a child, I reasoned like a child* . . . and the questions of faith and life that plague us all were most often put to rest by the confident creeds and dogmas of parents and a religious tradition rich in doctrine. And if I'm honest, I will admit that the certainties of faith and belief that shaped my early years still are formative in ways I don't always understand. Perhaps most of us can admit to the comfort and confidence of well-defined childhood faith.

But being curious and strong-willed and no doubt more than a little full of myself, it wasn't long until even a child rather smitten with religious ideas and issues began to challenge and question. Those summer forays exploring the islands around us and the depths below our leaky small skiff or the dark nights outside sleeping under the stars all played a part in the gathering momentum of doubt and questions. Together with age and ever-expanding experience, they both affirmed the wonder of the universe and confirmed a certain bewilderment about the complexities of the multifaceted, complicated world we call home.

Doubt and fear of the unknown are familiar companions. Most of us can recall childhood fears of the dark and the

ever-present doubts that nip at our heels and speak in the inter-
minable voices playing relentlessly in our heads. We all know the
weight of the world in the dark hours of the night when problems
of life seem insurmountable and where there is no going back to
the seeming simplicity of childhood. When the markers of certainty, those creeds we once professed with such confidence, no
longer work or when despair or hopelessness plunge us into darkness, then what? Can living with doubt and embracing darkness be
redemptive, life-giving? A benediction?

John of the Cross, a sixteenth-century Carmelite monk,
wrote from his prison cell in Spain (a place his order hoped would
silence him), that the dark night of the soul is God's best gift. By
this, John of the Cross did *not* mean that agony or angst are to be
venerated. He was not glorifying suffering nor did he mean, as has
been sometimes attributed to him, that doubt and darkness are
places of fear or despair. John of the Cross experienced liberation
in the darkness of his prison cell. He found there freedom from
our attachment to the doctrines, beliefs, and creeds that we think
will leave us feeling secure and closer to God. He found freedom
from all the ways we try to define God—freedom in uncertainty.
In the darkness of his exile, he learned to trust God in the absence
of certainty about God.

As in all of human history, we live in uncertain times. The
world is small and we know its fragile state all too well. Fear is
rampant today. It drives our society into a frenzy of traps we hope
will bring us longed for security and iron-clad safety. For many,
our facile attempts to find answers or solutions in religion no longer work. The God we may once have defined as *the way, the truth,
the life* is understood differently in other traditions and cultures
and the creeds we once confessed with such lock-step assurance
often feel outdated or strangely anachronistic. There seems to be
no permanently safe place to settle.

But might it be that in the midst of our angst, in the places
where we all hang on for dear life, new birth can take place? The
darkness of the night becomes the birthplace for a new day. Perhaps the certainties of childhood or even adulthood were not so

much about defining an indefinable God as they were about a system of beliefs that no longer works. If we are honest, we've known all along that God cannot be grasped or contained in words or pictures or doctrines. If we are honest, we know that *all* our feeble attempts to explain the sacred mystery of things are just that, woefully inadequate stabs at containing what cannot be contained.

With John of the Cross, I want to learn to trust God in the absence of certainty about God. I want to know the liberation he found in the darkness of his prison cell—freedom in uncertainty. Most of the time, that is enough. God's presence and what feels like God's absence can exist together. There are no precisely right words and no one tradition that nail it all down. I can live with that as a benediction. In the silence of a dark night and surrounded by a chaotic world that seems out of control, the undefinable mystery of God and God's holy presence is enough. That is benediction indeed.

REFLECTION

He found freedom from all the ways we try to define God—freedom in uncertainty. In the darkness of his exile, he learned to trust God in the absence of certainty about God.

* What does it mean that John of the Cross experienced liberation in the darkness of his prison cell?
* How do you understand doubt? Darkness?
* Does it make sense to you that God's presence and God's absence can exist together?
* How might doubt and darkness convey freedom?
* Is the undefinable mystery of God enough?

26

Good Company

She was extraordinary. We didn't speak one another's language and we were more than a generation apart in age. To communicate, we depended on the abilities of others to translate but we could sit together looking at family photos and with animated and sometimes silly body language and the intensity of our desire to understand one another, share a love of life and companionship that defied ordinary communication. At the astonishing age of 101, she was still good company.

He is a legend for his riveting interviews with interesting people from all walks of life. For several decades he has hosted a public television program that helps illuminate difficult issues, tackles moral and ethical questions, celebrates the arts, science, medicine, and sports—all showcasing lives that make a difference. His pleasure and intense interest in his guests is generous, infectious. He is good company both for those he interviews and for his audience.

We all know special people whose passion for life and attention to others is contagious. To be in their company is life-giving. They are gracious and grace-filled, exuding genuine curiosity and pleasure in their interactions. They see the world through eyes of hope no matter how discouraging or unrealistic this sometimes is. With generous spirits and an attitude of gratefulness, these are sought-after friends who acknowledge the good in others and readily seek it out. They are good company.

She is a gifted artist and writer. Her life has not been easy and she sometimes laments the maelstrom of chaos and disappointments that characterize all our lives. But she sees through eyes of faith and she carries on. She knows the holy mystery of simple, ordinary rituals, the ways in which God blesses the world with the commonplace and enters our lives in human and humble form. From her I continue to learn about and notice the holiness of everyday life, ordinary things.

With whom do you seek good company? In this tumultuous, chaotic world and in the cramped quarters of my own fears and insecurities and self-preoccupation, I find good company in this artist and writer, in the centenarian whose language and life are different from my own, in the stranger who leads me to places I might otherwise never go. Wherever we are, we walk on holy ground made sacred by bearing benedictions—being good company—to one another in words and actions that convey the essence of a God who is love. *God be with you and keep you. God's face shine on you and be gracious to you.*

I seek the good company of people and places where the spirit of a loving God is real and palpable. Because truth to tell and in spite of all our doubts and cynicism and skepticism, the one thing I know is that God is love. The one place where God's face is consistent and reliably present is where acts of love and mercy bring deep healing and wholeness. *And may God's presence be with you and give you peace.*

I look for leaders who show goodwill and act with empathy, whose generosity of spirit is apparent in the transparency, clarity, and consistency of their words and actions, who are not afraid. I seek friends whose good company is life-giving and life-changing. To be in their presence is to embrace a new lease on life and to experience joy, hope, mercy, peace. In doubt and darkness, in the rituals of the Sabbath, in the commonplace events of ordinary life, and in all the ways we practice resurrection, the blessings of good company become benedictions.

God be with you and keep you. May God's face shine on you and be gracious to you. And may God's presence be with you and give you peace. The blessed light be on you, light without and light within. May sunlight shine on you and warm your heart until it glows like a great fire so that a stranger or a friend may come and find warmth in you. May God always bless you, love you, keep you. And may the God of all hope fill you with joy and peace in believing, that you might abound in hope. Good company indeed! Benedictions indeed!

REFLECTION

Wherever we are, we walk on holy ground made sacred by bearing benedictions—by being good company—to one another in words and actions that convey the essence of a God who is love.

* With whom and with what do you keep good company?

* What do you experience in that place, with that person?

* How do you say what God is?

* How is that a benediction?

Bibliography

Cronin, Deborah K. *Holy Ground: Celtic Christian Spirituality.* Nashville: Upper Room, 1999. Appeared originally in Kuno Meyer's *Selections from Ancient Irish Poetry.* London: Constable, 1911.

Foley, John B. "One Bread, One Body." Hymn. Portland: Oregon Catholic Press, 1978.

Haugen, Marty. "As the Grains of Wheat." Hymn. Chicago: GIA, 1990.

———. "Now the Feast." Hymn. Chicago: GIA, 1990.

———. "Shepherd Me, O God." Hymn. Chicago: GIA, 1986.

Heschel, Abraham J. *Man Is Not Alone: A Philosophy of Religion.* New York: Farrar, Straus & Giroux, 1976.

James, William. From a letter to Thomas Ward, 1968. http://www.uky.edu/~eushe2/quotations/james.html.

Koperski, Veronica. "Holy Ground." Poem. First appeared in *Liturgy* 9.3 (1991); reprinted 1998.

Mueller Nelson, Gertrud. *Here All Dwell Free: Stories to Heal the Wounded Feminine.* New York: Paulist, 1999.

Peck, M. Scott. *The Different Drum.* New York: Simon & Schuster, 1987. This mythical story appears in many places and the source of the version here is obscure.

Pierpoint, Folliott S. "For the Beauty of the Earth." First appeared in *Lyra Eucharistica, Hymns and Verses on the Holy Communion,* 1864. Available at http://www.hymnsite.com/lyrics/umh092.sht.

Raines, Robert. *Creative Brooding.* New York: Macmillan, 1967. The story appeared originally in Loren Eiseley's *The Immense Journey.* New York: Random House, 1946.

Shea, John. *Stories of Faith.* Allen, TX: Thomas More, 1996.

Vajda, Jaroslav. "Go, My Children, with My Blessing." Hymn. St. Louis: CPH, 1983.